THE AGE
OF ROCOCO

Terisio Pignatti

THE AGE
OF ROCOCO

CASSELL
LONDON

Cassell Publishers Limited
Artillery House, Artillery Row
London SW1P 1RT

Translated by Lorna Andrade from the Italian original
Il Rococò

British Library Cataloguing in Publication Data

Pignatti, Terisio, *1920-*
The age of rococo. — (Cassell's styles in art).
1. European visual arts, 1700-1800 - Critical studies
I. Title   II. Il Rococo. *English*
709'.03'3

ISBN 0-304-32177-X

Printed in Italy by Gruppo Editoriale Fabbri, Milan

CONTENTS
Page

INTRODUCTION

It is widely held that the first half of the 18th century covers the period of the Rococo style. We can say without further ado that this popular view is substantially correct, but let us briefly consider the historical truth of the statement.

This period of history is extremely complex. Far-reaching political and social revolutions were taking place, and philosophers, scientists and artists brought their ideas to maturity in France, Italy, Germany, the Low Countries, England and Spain—in fact, in every European country. It would be impossible to gather together this wealth of material and to consider all of it as embodying the Rococo style, even in the narrowest sense of the term. The 18th century is a time of intense creativity both in spiritual and in practical matters, but these elude reduction to a lowest common denominator even in the figurative arts. This account is concerned solely with the arts and an attempt will be made to define the aspects shared by them all—

that is, their formal aims, stylistic practices and generally diffused forms, using the vast figurative vocabulary that one may call the language of the Rococo.

A brief glance at the geography of the arts in Europe in the first decade of the 18th century reveals an unusual panorama. It shows that the figurative language has evolved in a precise direction, whether in the graceful pavilions of the Trianon at Versailles, the arabesque-decorated rooms of the Hôtel de Soubise in Paris, the Sans-Souci palace in Potsdam, the Residency Theatre in Munich, the pale honey-coloured abbeys of Franconia or the brilliant gilded ornamentation of the altars in Munich. There is an undoubted connection between the Arcadian sweetness of Watteau's *Return from Cythera* and the beauty of Boucher's *Diana Bathing,* Pellegrini's *Rebecca* and Tiepolo's *Beauty Conquering Time,* a porcelain harlequin by Bustelli and a shepherdess in a Neapolitan crib, an engraving by Fragonard and the fairylike grotesques of Piranesi's *Capriccio Romano.*

The Europe of Diderot and Voltaire, Goldoni and Metastasio, Vivaldi and Bach shares a common inspiration, revealing itself in many local variations. The spirit of artists in different countries colours this common thread and changes the externals, but a similar imagination develops in similar directions. This is the language of the Rococo, the aesthetic movement uniting the figurative arts of 18th-century Europe, however diverse on the surface.

THE HISTORICAL MEANING OF THE WORD ROCOCO

'Rococo,' says the Dictionary of the French Academy in 1835, 'usually covers the kind of ornament, style and design associated with Louis XV's reign and the beginning of that of Louis XVI.' It includes, therefore, all aspects of art developed during the former reign—particularly about 1750—a period of economic and spiritual prosperity in France and famous for the work of the greatest artists.

But what is the origin of the word 'Rococo'? The words 'Baroque' and 'Rococo' are both used pejoratively by Neo-classical critics who objected to all the new art forms as being too eccentric and lacking in restraint. The true origin of the word 'Rococo' is conveyed by *rocaille* (rock-work, rockery). According to Kimball, one of the most learned modern critics, 'Rococo' is correctly employed from 1734 to indicate those kinds of ornament that remind one of *rocailles* (rocks) used in the decoration of gardens: small glittering rocks, shells to encrust grottoes and fountains, bringing out a dazzling light and grace. This art was born in France in the 16th century; in fact the artisans who practised it were known as *rocailleurs*. *Rocaille* was soon applied to a particular ornamental style developed in France at the beginning of the 18th century, first in interior architecture and then spreading to allied arts. The fundamental characteristic of this original French *rocaille* is the development of the line, which is cleverly twisted into curves, into shells and scrolls, applied on a surface such as mirrors or porcelain, with picturesque arabesques and light and gay motifs. This ornamentation becomes increasingly asymmetrical; and it is easy to foresee the development from such motifs towards more important creativity in the fields of painting and sculpture in France, for example, at the beginning of the 18th century.

FRENCH ROCOCO

A glance at the position of the arts in France is indispensable in order to understand the revolutionary change brought by Rococo as it developed. The change was so great that Rococo became known as *modern style* in contradistinction to the rather heavier Baroque style of the late 17th century. As always, what was new in French art centred round Louis XIV, the Sun King, and the court at Versailles. From 1699 Jules Hardouin Mansart, Superintendent of Buildings, had set on foot important plans for modernising both Versailles and the royal châteaux. Pierre Lepautre, designer of interiors under the direction of Mansart, decorated in 1699 various rooms at Marly and also at Meudon and the Trianon at Versailles. Many designs and engravings by Lepautre still exist. They show elegant fireplaces surrounded by *boiseries*, and here and there appear certain characteristic small leaves, already arranged in *rocaille* style. Academicians noticed this and sharply censured the *nouvelle manière*, which to them seemed faulty or downright 'Gothicised'! Meanwhile, the reform in decoration of royal palaces soon spread to the houses of the aristocracy in Paris. Artists working at Versailles, such as Lepautre and Vassé, were followed by Gilles Marie Oppenord and Boffrand. Their work for the Palais Royal, residence of Philip of Orléans, regent of France (1716), and for the Petit Luxembourg (1710) is an example of the by now perfected *rocaille* style; in luminously bright rooms white and gold triumph in the 'modern style', and scrolls, whorls and line arabesques pursue each other lightly along the cornice of wood panelling, in overmantels, overdoors and the curves of ceilings. The flowering of the decorative elements assumes from now onwards an abstract appearance of plant life, luxuriant foliage and scrolls; the line breaks up into a hundred sharp turns, and traditional symmetry is discarded in the frames for looking-glasses, tending towards a freer, more subtle and picturesque fancy. Apart from Oppenord's designs for the Palais Royal, examples of this period are Vassé's decorations for the Hôtel de Toulouse (1718-1719) destined to make their mark in the formation of the new language. Among the most important surviving decorative work of this period is that for the Hôtel de Bourvallais by de Cotte (1717) and for the Château de Chantilly (1722) by Jean Aubert, which is much richer than that of their immediate predecessors. Capricious arabesques rise from the ground, run along the architectural partitions of the walls, a fantastic gilded florescence outlining the panels, themselves enriched with painting by the greatest artists of the time.

During the regency of Philip of Orleans lasting until 1722 the foundations were laid for the era of the new decoration and furnishing of royal châteaux and houses of the nobility. Moreover the removal of the entire court from Versailles to Paris had caused a sort of rivalry amongst the great families, who employed scores of architects and decorators to alter in the *rocaille* style their smaller residences. Numerous books of engravings and ornamental *motifs* have come down to us from the beginning of the reign of Louis XV, first among them all being the famous work by the sculptor J.O. Meissonnier published in Paris in 1734. It is to Meissonnier, as well as to Pineau and Boucher, that we owe the beginning of the mature phase of French Rococo, developed in the years from 1730 to 1745. One thinks particularly of the superb chandeliers and table centres; but there are also plans for the altars of St Sulpice, treated as theatrical scenery, while Pineau created his masterpiece in the Hôtel de Matignon (1731). Here the branching decoration forming the surrounds of panelling achieved the delicate fancy sought in chinoiserie, which had recently become fashionable. Among what has survived is the characteristic decoration of the Hôtel de Soubise by Boffrand (1736), where even the internal space of the small rooms seems to lend itself to the floral vegetation of *rocaille,* multiplying points of view with perspectives created by mirrors, doors and windows, in an inexhaustible play of fantasy and elegance.

But the new generation of architects and decorators, headed by J. A. Gabriel, soon reacted against excessively rich decoration and used a more restrained and less broken line, foreshadowing the Neo-classical reaction.

This is a general outline of the development and formation of the Rococo in France during the first fifty years of the 18th century. It is unnecessary to discuss in detail the amazing genius of the artists who contributed to this figurative process for they are included in *Louis XV,* also in this series. It is enough briefly to recall the first designers of painted panelling, such as Audran and Gillot, and above all Watteau, who personifies the deeply refined spirit of the age in many paintings illustrating in his *fêtes galantes* members of the aristocracy engaged in pleasure. Favourite painter of Madame de Pompadour, the king's mistress, was Boucher, master of the art of transporting into small Parisian boudoirs the gay sensual world of mythology. The many artists in the field of sculpture and in every kind of interior *rocaille* decoration defy description: the delicate Falconet, the caustic Houdon, the refined and sensual Clodion. Many of them worked for the Sèvres and Fontainebleau factories, and enriched porcelain with original and attractive designs.

Around the masters of the more important arts

there moved in the France of the Rococo a whole world of decorators and craftsmen skilled in making furniture. Among the most famous were Cressent, Gaudreaux, Oeben and Riesener, and the anonymous craftsmen who made the Gobelins, Beauvais and Aubusson tapestries and worked to the designs prepared for them by contemporary painters.

THE SPIRIT OF THE ROCOCO IN EUROPE

This vigorous creative activity had changed the taste in decoration, and a new language was born covering every form of artistic work. Research in the many spheres of intellectual life as it affected artists would be interesting, because they often drew their inspiration from the intellectual climate. A profound change had come about in the field of culture, and in particular in philosophy, even influencing ideas about life itself. In the days of the Sun King no one had questioned the value of an absolutist hierarchy, under which every form of material and intellectual activity was concentrated round the court. This same philosophy with its ordered rationalism gave validity to the hypothesis of a preordained world with infallible laws. Now, however, the philosophy of sensationalism, introduced at the beginning of the 18th century with the theories of Locke, Hume and Berkeley, cast doubt on these convictions. The resulting speculation prepared the ground for the philosophic enlightenment that was to give new life to France in the middle of the century. The *Encyclopedia* of Diderot and Montesquieu, published in 1751, crowned a whole era of research and new ideals.

Thus, liberal theories and ideas about natural right triumphed over transcendentalism, and it is easy to understand what were the practical results in the life of society, in manners and in art. Culture, too, now more widely diffused, prepared the way for new behaviour and new forms in the arts; Rococo became a European fact, and the courts spread it throughout Europe. At the very end of the age in which the idea of 'divine right' was supreme, it is curious that the Rococo was the generally accepted expression of the society that had dominated Europe in the preceding century.

In imitation of Versailles and the châteaux of the kings of France many fine houses were built in every part of Europe—from those by Juvarra at Turin and Stupinigi to Caserta by Vanvitelli, from houses at Würzburg and Pommersfelden in Franconia to Schleissheim, and also at Nuremberg in Bavaria, Ludwigsburg in Württemberg, Sans-Souci in Prussia and the Belvedere at Schönbrunn near Vienna. All the courts of Europe looked towards France and took up in one way or another her artists and her ideas of decoration.

In these courts there was an unceasing, lively cultural exchange, specially in the French-inspired manners of daily life, and thus the language of the figurative arts was being constantly diffused. Much of the most important work was in the designs for *fêtes,* concerts, balls and grandiose theatrical entertainments. Groups of stage designers were continually producing new dramatic spectacles, and they all contributed to the standardisation of its vocabulary. The Bibiena family revitalised stage decoration, with their new effects in perspective; and Juvarra, Servandoni, Fossati and Galliera were accepted by the whole art world of Europe and staged public entertainments of an unimaginable splendour. Amongst others were the pompous celebrations for the marriage of the Prince Elector of Saxony for which the court for four weeks during 1719 employed a host of artists at Dresden. Allegorical performances, processions, balls, masked entertainments, in which even the royal bride and bridegroom took part, followed one another in a specially created environment.

For these court festivities the interior decorations were frequently influenced by oriental taste, and we find mentions of Japanese pavilions and of Turkish, and even Siberian, costumes. The passion of the century was for travel, and this passion, allied to the fantasy of artists, helped in the invention of ever new ornamental themes. Orientalism is moreover a characteristic enthusiastically taken up by Rococo artists, who saw in chinoiserie a form akin to the taste for the picturesque, the capricious, the architecturally light: English Rococo reveals this taste in Chippendale furniture.

Another aspect of the Rococo period, derived from fashionable festivities, was a passionate presentation of life in Arcadia. On the one hand bucolic poetry was cultivated, the verse cadences reminiscent of Arcadia; on the other there sprang up in France societies of gallants (called *sociétés d'amour*) differentiated by such significant names as 'The Gallant Academy', 'The Honey-Bee Society' and 'The Society of Aphrodite'. Most popular of all were poems with Arcadian subjects or passages from Ovid's *Metamorphoses*. The Daphnis and Chloe myth had the honour of a de luxe edition, supervised in person by the regent, Philip of Orléans, in 1718! The theme of the return to nature, the charm of pastoral life and the sugar-sweet innocence of shepherd girls and boys offered an infinite number of subjects to the painters of the time, above all to Boucher who portrays them in his exquisite canvases framed in *boiseries*. (One remembers the enchanting *Salle de Madame Pompadour,* formerly in the Château de Crécy and now in the Frick Collection, New York.) This theme of pastoral Arcadia inspired a whole generation of painters working in every part of Europe in the orbit of the Rococo, and these motifs particularly influenced the Venetians, from Rosalba Carriera to the landscape painters Zais and Zuccarelli. One of the Rococo's most characteristic poetic subjects, that of love, is expressed in Arcadian and pastoral painting. Already from the beginning of the century many of the old gods of Olympus had been ousted by a few who symbolised aspects of gallantry—

Venus and Pan, Diana the Huntress and Cupid. With the passing of time the motif of gallantry became more direct and intimate, being used in downright equivocal bourgeois situations. Elderly husbands sleep while a young wife slips a letter to her lover; a kiss is snatched surreptiously at the door of a theatre box; a love-sick youth glances indiscreetly at the bathroom of his beloved; a shepherd tickles a girl with milk-white complexion as she lies deep in slumber . . . Even the most intimate scenes in daily life are exposed in innumerable paintings and engravings illustrated in books that are masterpieces of the 18th century; the bedroom becomes an accepted centre of a religion of nature, founded on the pleasures of the senses, and all modesty is abandoned. All this is in harmony with the age; weary of the solemn theatricality of the 17th century, the artist of the Rococo imposes his theory of 'intimacy' in its most sensual and gay aspects as a hymn to nature's freedom. The position of figurative art, for so long closely associated with religion, was curious. On the one hand, particularly in painting, there is the insistent return of Baroque themes exalting the deity and its celestial triumphs, and on the other, even in the work of the most celebrated artists, one detects those intimate, sensual nuances found in life itself and vainly masked by conventional trappings, manners and behaviour. One thinks of the great paradisiacal celebrations by a Tiepolo in Venice or a Maulbertsch in Austria, and of the sculpture in wood by Günther in Bavaria. Here, hardly concealed, are all the gay, spirited caprices of the era—crinolines, gallant cavaliers, powdered ladies. Works of art, even in their rhetorical and flamboyant religiosity, made use of the same basic language as that of artists more deeply inspired by Rococo themes.

In the field of religious architecture, apparently little influenced by *rocaille*, one finds a complete change from the religious representation characteristic of the Baroque to something more intimate, demanding the understanding and cooperation of modern man. The rooms of the huge abbeys in south Germany seem now to draw their inspiration from the intimacy of private drawing-rooms in daily use; every effort is made to suggest the refined beauty and bizarre grace to be found in any aristocratic home of the Rococo period, such as rooms decorated with mirrors, a series of fireplaces, and ceilings ornate with arabesques.

In conclusion, the spiritual environment in which the figurative motifs of the Rococo developed, first in France and then in Europe, is entirely different from that which saw the development of Baroque art in the 17th century. The changes that took place in culture, philosophy, literature, music and scientific principles broke down the barriers, hitherto respected, between the world of the spirit and that of the senses. The importance of the individual in the art of the time is shown in an infinite variety of original work by hundreds of creative artists, favoured by a social climate in which the need for outward visible change ran parallel with the cultural renaissance. New themes

in the figurative arts of the Rococo formed the basis
for a common idiom. How they developed was determined by different historical backgrounds. The forms
taken by the Rococo in the various countries of
Europe will now be analysed in detail.

THE ROCOCO IN ITALY

The first years of the 18th century showed, in Italy as
in France, the beginning of that formal revolution
which soon expressed itself in the European idiom of
the Rococo. Italy was divided into numerous states,
each with an age-old political structure, many of
which had developed independent artistic cultures.
In this connection, the positions in Piedmont, Venice,
Rome and Naples were particularly interesting. In
each case the art of the early 18th century, as the result
either of direct influence or of gradual change, followed the new trends, whether spiritual or purely
decorative, of French Rococo culture. In Italy, as in
France, aristocratic society showed itself more liberal
and free from prejudice, more cultivated than formerly
and bent on a gay and pleasant life. In consequence,
many of the declamatory and rhetorical characteristics
of the Baroque were soon abandoned. Bold inventions
found expression in spectacular wild fancies and ever-
changing graceful caprices. In the early 18th century
Italian art became a faithful mirror of the frivolous
and elegant world: villas and palaces were comfortably

furnished, ornamented with charming knick-knacks and frescoed with 'bourgeois' subjects.

The brilliant cultural and artistic rebirth in 17th-century Piedmont reached its height in the first decades of the 18th century under the dukes of Savoy with the work of Filippo Juvarra, an architect who illustrates to perfection the European Rococo movement while yet retaining a typically Italian personality. His great merit was to know how to select from the traditions of the previous century those elements which could best be adapted to the new European sensibility, and to put aside the whole decorative lumber that, specially in north Italy, had made Italian Baroque heavy. Juvarra looked above all to Borromini, one of the fathers of the Rococo. In this way the most subtle and effective elements in 17th-century architecture were put to use.

Juvarra's early years were spent in Rome, where he lived from 1705 to 1714, working under Carlo Fontana. While he welcomed the classical motifs of the 17th century, his instinctive richness of invention made him more in sympathy with Borromini, who inspired him above all by his dynamic sense of structure and his bold yet sensitive ornament, restricted almost entirely to surfaces, as was usual with French artists of the *rocaille*. In his gift for design he was also encouraged by the education he had received from his father, a silversmith. He later devoted himself to theatrical design, following the Bibiena family, and showed a lively understanding of perspective.

On his return to Turin in 1714 he was appointed court architect at the very moment when Vittorio Amedeo II undertook his vast programme of urban reconstruction. For the next twenty years he turned his attention to this task and Turin took on a new appearance in line with European culture.

Juvarra's first important building in Turin was the basilica of the Superga (1716-1731), destined to be the mausoleum of the family of the dukes of Savoy. It is a complex construction harmonising the various components of the architect's culture. Placed on a raised foundation on the summit of a hill the church forms the advanced spur of an elaborate building with three wings. The portico leading to the cupola is in classical style, but the latter, raised above a second storey, is flanked to the north and south by gay little campaniles, reminiscent in many ways of the genius of Borromini. Thus the imposing building gives a Rococo impression of dramatic lightness, by means of the complicated play of light and perspective obtained from various viewpoints. The contemporary façade of Sta Cristina in Turin is another building which, starting from Roman-influenced elements, shows in full measure Juvarra's brilliance in new architectural forms. Upon a traditional, curving façade Juvarra imposed a new and rich decoration. The faceted pedestals of the statues accentuate the broken lines of the cornice and give a calculated vivacity to the church's theatrical appearance which, with the artifice of candelabras placed on the roof, appear to pay homage to childhood memories of altars decorated by his father's silversmiths's work.

Juvarra built many palaces in Turin: the della Valle, the d'Ormea, the Belgrano and, lastly, the most imposing, the Palazzo Madama. Here he had to add to the old castle fronting the piazza an entrance hall, grand staircase and a first floor gallery. The problem of illuminating the grand staircase is solved by a new technique. The two flights of stairs receive light from the open gallery. The decorative details are of the finest and the architect seems to bend the structure to its functional use. He is not only successful in the decoration but achieves an impressive, typically Rococo vigour. His technical skill allied to fantasy in construction are characteristic of the work of Juvarra's last years. The Scala delle Forbici (Scissor Staircase) is a restrained but fine example of a double flight of stairs bordered by a series of rising arches in a somewhat circumscribed well-shaft, and the design has superb ornamental features; the stairs seem to have been carved out a plastic structure, so great is the architectural suggestion of movement.

Juvarra's masterpiece is the hunting lodge at Stupinigi, built for Charles Emanuel III (1729-1733). The king wanted a villa with pavilions, as a place of meeting during stag hunts, which the guests attended in hunting costume, and the entire structure of this beautiful building was designed for this purpose. The most important feature, as in shown by numerous drawings, is the reception hall in the centre of four wings forming a St Andrew's cross. Two wings, low and very much prolonged, are reserved for guests and servants. Simple and bright perspectives greet the visitors in the court of honour, and the galaxy of statues and candelabras on the balconies adds a lively note. The interior, skilfully frescoed by the Valeriani with a *Diana at the Hunt,* gives the appearance of a theatre, offering from wing to wing, by the harmonius use of space, continual surprises from unusual and unexpected viewpoints. There are delightful little salons and romantic corners adjoining fireplaces and opening from the galleries. It is not easy to imagine a piece of architecture more suitable for the gay ceremonies for huntsmen of the nobility and their ladies, guests of the king. Juvarra made use of great decorative refinement and endless fantasy to complete the apartments in the wings. There were little rooms decorated with frescoes by Crosato and van Loo; and fine stucco-work for overdoors and windows gives a definitely Rococo impression to the mellow and welcoming surroundings.

The Stupinigi palace and the princely residences of the Trianon, Potsdam, Nymphenburg and Würzburg are among the most poetic architectural monuments of the Rococo and owe much to Juvarra's art of fantasy.

No other Italian architect working in the Rococo period equals Juvarra in artistic and cultural importance. A little later, however, we find an interesting school of architects in Piedmont, amongst them Alfieri and Vittone. In their work, façades capriciously curved, niches and the centralised plans all bring about a lively play of chiaroscuro and effects characteristic of the Rococo idiom. In numerous palaces in Lombardy, too, we find a sensitivity to light airy decoration, in particular in the Palazzo Mezzabarba by Veneroni in Pavia and in the work of M. Bianchi and the Sartori family.

Roman architects made an imposing contribution to the 18th-century appearance of that city. With Specchi and de Sanctis, who designed the dramatic Spanish Steps, Filippo Raguzzini (1675-1771) is remembered as the most original, specially in the lay-out of the Piazza St'Ignazio, where a broken line offers viewpoints, perspectives and surprises, and uses the capricious design of façade and cornices in Rococo fashion to dominate the conception. Other famous architects, such as Galilei, designer of the façade of S. Giovanni in Laterano, and Fuga, who carried out the building of Sta Maria Maggiore, show a curious mixture of Baroque taste and of the coming Neo-classical inspiration: their relationship with the Rococo idiom seems therefore only superficial. The great Piranesi, who liked to call himself an architect even if almost his only architectural achievement was the Malta Priory in Rome, was encouraged in his activities by Rococo influences. In his first engravings, published under the name of *Capricci,* the picturesque invention takes on all the grotesque forms, unexpected and elusive, of *rocaille* arabesques. Independent of Rococo culture, too, is Vanvitelli (1700-1773) who, in his royal palace of Caserta, organises grandiose Baroque effects in an architecture of dynamic space and strongly accented rhythms. There is no doubt that by its imposing conception Caserta bears comparison with the greatest creations of its kind. The most successful parts are those in which Vanvitelli seeks to equal by his architecture the overwhelming decorative richness of painting in Naples and Rome. The park is most important with its grand cascade, adorned with statues by Persico, Violani and Brunelli, with subjects from the chase and mythology. The green of the gardens is enhanced by water gaily flowing between white marble groups suggesting scenes from Arcadian life so familiar in Rococo art.

In Venice, in comparison with the complexity and richness of Venetian painting, local 18th-century architecture plays a secondary role. But there is a definite inclination towards the Rococo style in the buildings of Antonio Gaspari (1670-1730). By bringing to Venice the first influences of Borromini, which elsewhere were decisive in the formation of the Rococo language, he has the merit of having shown his contemporaries a means of overcoming timid 16th-century classicism. Few of his numerous projects were carried out; but his elegant Sta Maria must be remembered, with its interior rich in refined grace and decorated like a secular room with stucco and reliefs.

Gasperi's elegance calls to mind the second greatest

architect of Venetian Rococo, Giogio Massari (1686-1766) who in 1746 built the church of I Gesuati (Jesuits).

This chef-d'oeuvre of the Venetian 18th century owes its fascination to the frescoes by Tiepolo and to the sculpture by Morlaiter. It manages to achieve singular harmony in its complexity. All the decorative details in shimmering colour produce an atmosphere of 18th-century domestic interiors.

ITALIAN PAINTING OF THE ROCOCO

In those regions of Italy where the Baroque tradition remained strongest, the change in painting acquired individual characteristics. In Naples, Emilia and Venice the persistence of the 17th-century tradition made the evolution of the Rococo more difficult. Francesco Solimena, although he adopted lighter forms, remains an exponent of the Baroque. In the marvellous frescoes in S. Paolo Maggiore the young Solimena painted a series of attractive portraits, rich in colour, which were to prove important in the development of the 18th-century school of painting in Naples, where the gifted del Po, de Mura and Giaquinto lived and worked.

The Neapolitan school flowered in an ideal climate. There existed a considerable figurative culture, determined amongst other things by the architectural activity of Vanvitelli and by southern Italian sculptors such as Vaccaro and Corradini and the Sicilian Serpotta. Corrado Giaquinto (1699-1765), an important artist, created works of ethereal lightness and grace, approximating in nuances of colour to the Rococo. Perhaps even more delicate is the decorative genius of Francesco de Mura (1696-1792) who worked in Piedmont after 1730. Even if these artists lacked the social and intellectual background for the achievement of an authentic Rococo art, 18th-century Naples fills an important position in European art history. Much Italian painting early in the century tends to echo 17th-century tradition. Not that artists were limited by this tendency; some of the greatest of them absorbed it and thereby enhanced their work.

Vittore Ghislandi was not a reactionary though his inspiration can be clearly traced to the 17th-century Bombelli and to Salomone Adler. Through them Ghislandi was able to go back to the sources of European painting, to van Dyck and Rembrandt, and to achieve a 'European' significance. Typical of Ghislandi is his realism, enabling him to convey in his beautiful portraits psychological introspection as well as a critical analysis of the individual in his relation to society. His cruel and empty-headed *Gentiluomini,* as in the painting of Poldo Pezzoli, resemble portraits of monks and youths, and they surprise by their realism and pictorial actuality.

A position of isolation is characteristic of some Italian painters of the first half of the 18th century, but

Ghislandi's art cannot be described as provincial. It is capable of arousing spiritual emotions that range from the art of Rembrandt to the philosophy of sensationalism of Locke, Hume and Condillac. Nor can another important painter, Giuseppe Maria Crespi, be described as provincial although he spent his whole life in his native city of Bologna and worked in isolation. The great 17th-century tradition passed before his eyes, from Carracci to Guercino, from Burrini to Pasinelli, from Canuti to Cignani. But Crespi's genius expressed itself in a highly individual manner; he selected from that world, rich with colour and movement, subjects from life for the famous *Fiera di Poggia a Cajano* (Fair at Poggia) and for his *Sacramenti* (Seven Sacraments); little everyday scenes such as *La Pulce* (The Flea) in the Uffizi and even for his portraits. He used colour as an independent language, capable of showing with intense realism the relationship between art and nature.

Unbelievable though it may seem, it is through the study of Crespi's sharply defined and glowing colour schemes that other Venetian painters of the early 18th century, such as Piazzetta and Longhi, learned once more the true use of colour.

Giambattista Piazzetta, for example, could not be explained were it not that as a young man in Bologna he had studied Crespi, and this was decisive for his development. Even a certain lavishness in the use of warm, sunlit, iridescent colour goes back to the Bolognese painter, though Piazzetta may combine these with the richer colour harmonies of the 18th-century Venice of Johann Liss and Fetti. But because of his education in the 'grand manner' of the Baroque, Piazzetta cannot claim a decisive position in the formation of the new figurative vocabulary of the 18th century. He seems somewhat backward-looking, a solemn yet most honourable *laudator temporis acti*. In any case he was a great artist, and it must be remembered that among the apprentices in his studio the very young Tiepolo worked, learning there the use of colour and freeing himself from the danger of an apprenticeship to Lazzarini, a survivor from the most mediocre period of 17th-century Venice. Piazzetta's influence was strong even on the young Austrian painters of the generation of Troger and Maulbertsch.

To return to the main current of European art. Travelling Venetian painters illustrate a particular aspect of the Rococo; in the first decade of the 18th century they had already spread in Europe the idea of fresh, graceful painting, fluent in design, attractive and light in musical invention, a reflection of the joy of living. Pellegrini, Ricci and Amigoni used a special vocabulary, approximating to that used in France, to give laws to Europe until the end of the century. Giovanni Antonio Pellegrini was the first to leave Venice for London, where we find him in 1708. He peopled sombre English castles with mythological figures, softened by an Arcadian atmosphere, with dreams in blue and rose, with the gay, graceful rhythms of an 'arietta'. In London, Pellegrini, a very young follower of Luca Giordano, had rediscovered van Dyck who was to mean a great deal in the revival of French art, and had reintroduced his qualities of lightness of touch, unexpected imaginative flights, airy frivolity and iridescent light. Pellegrini remained in London until 1713 and then went to Düsseldorf (1713-1716), to Holland (1716-1718) and to Paris (1719-1720). In Germany his masterpieces are the canvases for the Elector William, now at Schleissheim, in which the figures are treated with the greatest sensitivity.

Sebastiano Ricci was older than Pellegrini, but from the first he was influenced by a purely 18th-century poetic spirit. Versed in the great tradition of Naples and the Carracci, he was a superb decorative artist and overcame by his virtuosity an almost insuperable academic obstacle, the temptation to marry traditional designs with the refined and musical art of the 18th century. His model became—and continued to be—the great Paolo Veronese. He, too, had much experience of Europe: he went to London in 1712 and then to Holland and Paris (1717). With Ricci a solid vein of Venetian colour permeated European culture, specially important in German-speaking countries where he was much imitated, and in Germany the teaching of Jacopo Amigoni (1717-1725) was significant. Later he worked in England (1730-1739) and in Spain, where he died. He is the least important of the three painters mentioned but also perhaps the easiest to imitate. In his work traditional forms of late Venetian and Neapolitan Baroque are softened by Arcadian voluptuousness; it retains, too, a moderate classicism and a certain dignified balance. The activity of Venetian painters increased during the first twenty years of the 18th century, a period corresponding with the regency of Philip of Orléans which ushered in the Rococo.

Various portrait painters come to mind here who gave an individual slant to European painting. They influenced other artists by their international outlook and their precise documentation on costume and manners. First is Rosalba Carriera, Venetian by birth but nevertheless a citizen of Europe. Her early education was due not so much to local masters as to her work in the studios of late Baroque artists such as Giordano or 'international' painters such as Pellegrini (her brother-in-law), taking us to the centre of the main currents of Rococo taste. Rosalba Carriera took from them not only their clear iridescent colours but also the spectacular self-assurance, the elaborate bravura and the subtle, slightly malicious spirit which opened to her the doors of the aristocracy in Europe. From the beginning of the 18th century the most distinguished personalities of the international *beau monde* were to be met in Rosalba's studio. Some came to have their portraits painted, others to buy series of pastel drawings to adorn their sumptuous palaces in far-off countries. Christian of Mecklenburg, Frederick of Denmark and the Elector of Dresden are illustrious proof of Rosalba's fame. From 1720 to 1721 she was

1. Antoine Watteau (1684-1721). *The Assembly in the Park.*
c. 1717. Louvre, Paris.

2. François Boucher (1703-1770). *Diana Resting.* 1742.
Louvre, Paris.

3. Gian Battista Piazzetta (1683-1754). *Idyll on the Shore.*
c. 1740. Wallraf-Richartz Museum, Cologne.

4. Giovanni Antonio Pellegrini (1675-1741). *Marriage of the Elector William.* 1714. The palace, Schleissheim.

5. Giovanni Antonio Pellegrini (1675-1741). *Painting. c.* 1730.
The Accademia, Venice.

6. Sebastiano Ricci (1659-1734). *Hercules and Cacus.* 1706-1707. Palazzo Marucelli, Florence.

7. Rosalba Carriera (1675-1757). *Faustina Bordoni. c.* 1730.
Ca' Rezzonico, Venice.

8. Louis Tocqué (1696-1772). *The Comtesse Loménie de Brienne.* 1737. Musée des Beaux-Arts, Strasbourg.

9. Gian Battista Tiepolo (1696-1770). *Rinaldo Charmed by Armida. c.* 1753. Alte Pinakothek, Munich.

10. Francesco Guardi (1712-1793).
The Convent Parlour. c. 1750.
Ca' Rezzonico, Venice.

11. Gian Antonio Guardi
(1699-1760). *Tobit and his Wife
in Prayer* (detail). *c.* 1749.
Church of the Arcangelo
Raffaele, Venice.

12. Gian Battista Tiepolo (1696-1770). The Orlando Furioso Room (1757). Villa Valmarana, Vicenza.

13. Pietro Longhi (1702-1782). *The Charlatan*. 1757. Ca' Rezzonico, Venice.

14. Giovan Paolo Pannini (1692-1765). *Charles III Visiting St Peter's.* 1745. Capodimonte Museum, Naples.

15. Antonio Canal, known as Canaletto (1697-1768). *The Piazza of S. Marco.* National Gallery of Art, Washington.

16. Francesco Guardi (1712-1793). *The Little Piazza of S. Marco. c.* 1765. Ca' d'Oro, Venice.

in Paris where her success was undisputed. Famous painters discussed her portraits and Coypel, Rigaud, Mariette and Caylus praised them. She painted Watteau's portrait and he gave her one of his own paintings. In this period, which lasted until nearly 1740, Rosalba's technique reached its greatest refinement. Certain shades of blue and pearl-grey merge into an amber-coloured luminescence, and Coypel was justified in comparing her with Correggio in her picture *Girl with a Dove* in the Louvre. This was the European ideal in painting and Rosalba was among its finest exponents. To the soft shades of the painter's palette Rosalba added richness in psychological insight and an ingenious capacity for penetrating beneath the surface: it is enough to mention *Faustina Bordoni*, *Polignac* in Venice or *Metastasio* in Vienna, truly individual portraits from the point of view of the period. Struck down by cataract, Rosalba gradually became blind. This disaster affected her whole life, and her painting changed. It became sombre, almost dismal in colouring, as in her last tragic self-portraits in the art galleries of London and Venice. 'I can't see anything any more. It is as if I am surrounded by night,' she wrote in 1749 to Mariette. From then onwards, suffering and unhappy, her mind weakened. She died blind in 1757. Her poetic gifts did not fail to make an impression throughout Europe.

Typically Venetian in the delicate harmonies of her palette, Rosalba had interpreted aspects of international Rococo with such skill that she had many imitators. First among them was the Frenchman La Tour, a good psychologist, and showing great artistic talent in his pastels, which shine with luminous cool colour. Between 1730 and 1750 La Tour was the recognised portrait painter of French high society, the favourite of Madame de Pompadour, arbiter in Parisian art politics. More subtle, and perhaps a truer artist, was his rival J. B. Perronneau, but the latter could never wholly overcome a certain restricting academicism in his rich but mannered painting, which had the characteristic dignity of the earlier period. The Swiss painter Jean Etienne Liotard may also be included among the host of pastel portraitists following in Rosalba's wake. His realism is Dutch in origin, reminiscent perhaps of Vermeer. He paid the greatest attention to details of costume and background and produced some vivid contemporary portraits. He completed the group of portrait painters of international repute, striving—even in their use of pastel technique—towards an intimate interpretation of character rather than towards a traditional portrait in the grand manner.

Other great portrait painters should be mentioned who have a connection with this period of European Rococo. About the middle of the century Jean Marc Nattier came to the fore. He succeeded in combining the verve of the Rococo with the magnificence of the Franco-Flemish tradition.

With these masters French culture was getting ready to impose itself over the greater part of Europe.

After Nattier, who frequently visited Holland and central Europe, came the more important Tocqué. He carried French influence even to Russia and the countries of the north. One of the most significant chapters in the century's culture covers the phenomenon of the diffusion of French art in the middle of the 18th century. While Venice sent abroad one or two painters of the first rank, from Paris whole companies of first class artists and craftsmen moved to the conquest of Europe. There was no castle, no palace, no famous collection where Frenchmen were not to be found, while in Rome the French Academy became the centre of cultural attraction both for amateurs and for young artists. Further, Italian courts in Tuscany, Parma and Piedmont, where van Loo and Beaumont worked, were open to French taste and fashion. In Germany an extraordinary flowering of castles and palaces enriched 18th-century art, and their decoration was entirely in French hands, whether in Karlsrühe, Mannheim or Düsseldorf. The painting of the most famous German portrait painter, George des Marées, working in Munich and Bonn, echoed the style of the Frenchman Pesne.

At times, this 'Frenchifying' depended on the personality of the reigning monarch: in Berlin, Queen Charlotte took Versailles as her model; in Prussia, at Potsdam, Frederick II employed Pesne and van Loo. The interiors of their palaces are very rich in work by the greatest French artists. The collections of paintings by Watteau, Pater and Lancret, made by

Frederick II, show the predominance of the *rocaille* style in the decoration of German architecture.

In Austria, van Schuppen, a pupil of Largillière, founded the Academy of Fine Arts; in Christianborg in Denmark the palace is hung with pictures commissioned in Paris from Lancret, Oudry, Parrocel, de Troy and Natoire. It was the same in Stockholm where the royal palace was decorated by Taraval.

Giuseppe Bazzani (1690-1769) from Mantua, who looked principally to the great Venetian masters from Ricci to G. A. Guardi, was an independent artist, but certainly familiar with the prestige of Rococo in Europe. His spirited figures of saints, many of which are still in the churches of his native province, glow with colour and are painted with rapid touches and lively rhythm. Finally, two Venetians, Gian Antonio Guardi and Gian Battista Tiepolo, among the greatest painters of the Rococo, seem to complete this cycle of 18th-century art.

Gian Antonio Guardi has only relatively recently been discovered and appreciated, but there is no doubt that he must be considered as one of the greatest artists of the final period of Rococo history. Unlike his masters Guardi did not have the good fortune to travel in Europe. He worked first in Vienna, his birthplace, and in Val di Non, Trentino, the land of his ancestors, and finally in Venice.

Orphaned when young, he had as his first assistants his much younger brothers, Francesco and Nicolo. From 1730 to 1740 he was principally occupied in copying old paintings for Venetian collectors, such as the Giovannelli family and Marshal Schulenberg. Transplanted from the upper Adige to Venice this painter was content just to earn a bare living. Probably he was meanwhile finding his bearings in his new surroundings. There were too many geniuses around him, and too many well known artists travelling round the world, so it is easy to understand why riches eluded him. Gian Antonio's first work, however, fits immediately into the tradition of Rococo painting. In his only signed canvas, the *Death of Joseph*, the extraordinary quality of the colour shows that this is the work of a great artist. Beneath his brush matter itself seems to break up, dissolving in the light into thousands of silver and gold flecks. Some of his blues have the crystalline quality of lapis lazuli, while the transparency of clothing creates a sort of subtle harmony, a music of strings, revealing even more sharply the delicate outlines of the design, sensitive, tender, minutely detailed. No one interpreted better than Guardi the themes and style of the Rococo.

Gian Antonio's masters are Pellegrini, for his silky, delicate colour, and Ricci, whose manner is recognisable in Guardi's plastic construction and his figures. There is, too, a basic Nordic element due, on his father's side, to his Viennese origin and education — a use of sparkling colour and a more nervous touch that are at the roots of Bavarian sculpture, such as that of Günther and Tietz in certain garden statues, delightfully introduced into the green ambience of parks.

Formed by divers influences, Gian Antonio achieves a unity of personality and a musical freshness of language. His Cini *Aurora* and the *Diana* at the Ca' Rezzonico, more than any other paintings of the mid 18th century, can create the climate—all charm and tenderness—of the Venice of the time. Only Rosalba Carrera had used such beautiful brushwork which in Guardi has the breadth of a Largo by Handel.

Gian Antonio Guardi died in 1760 after having painted that extraordinary cantoria (singers' gallery) in the church of the Arcangelo Raffaelo. Here by virtuoso technique paint dissolves into a golden fantasy of light, refracting, crossing, superimposed. Mythical figures move in an almost surrealist atmosphere. Nothing remains of the traditional attitude to landscape painting, and we get an impression of pure, stimulating colour.

Gian Antonio Guardi is the most independent personality of the last period of European Rococo. With him we have, even in Venice, crossed the mid century barrier. The parabola launched by Pellegrini fifty years earlier has come full circle. Only Tiepolo remains who, by his greatness, stands alone and cannot be omitted from any European panorama of the Rococo.

Gian Battista Tiepolo, born in Venice at the end of the 17th century, had the advantage of finding himself from the very beginning in a climate free from the last heavy restraints of the Baroque. In the first twenty years of the 18th century Sebastiano Ricci and G. A.

Pellegrini, who created the new Rococo taste in painting, had worked in Venice. When, therefore, between 1715 and 1720 the young Tiepolo came into the limelight (even if his probable masters were Bencovich and Piazzetta, still using the dark 'lights' of the 17th century) he was drawn towards great decorative painting, bright and melodious, in the great tradition of the European Rococo. This irresistible call to the gifted artist showed itself towards the end of the third decade. After 1730 Tiepolo diverged from Piazzetta (in spite of the latter's endeavours to get rid of the gloominess of his altarpieces—impressive but conservative in spirit) and set out on the path of Ricci and Pellegrini. He gathered universal praise, attracted to himself all the commissions from the nobility and the Church and became their favourite artist.

Even if it were against his will, Tiepolo took up the position of 'state painter' of the two classes dominating the social world. His choice of subjects, religious and secular, his complex and formal perspectives, his marked tendency towards the grand manner (and to working quickly) are not among the most positive aspects of the prevailing culture; but his support of courtly and apparently superficial rhetoric is in his case allied to a genuine revival of the great Venetian tradition of the 16th century and above all is inspired by Paolo Veronese.

The 'luminous' Veronese presented Tiepolo, his young successor, with an unrivalled example of decorative fantasy, and Tiepolo attempted a renaissance of the glorious golden age of Venetian painting. He endeavoured to portray the 18th-century descendants of Veronese's 16th-century patrons with the same luminous grandeur in composition and colour. There is no question of Neo-classicism in the years between 1730 and 1750 when he reached the highest point in his career. For Tiepolo the iridescent colour harmonies of Ricci's later work and Pellegrini's opalescent light meant more than the frivolous charm of the Rococo, as is shown in the Udine frescoes of 1726-1728, his first masterpiece. Nor was Tiepolo unaware of the liveliness and sweetness of Rosalba's pastels as can be seen from his charcoal drawings and his Scuola dei Carmini canvases of about 1740 with their milky glow. But his adherence to the Rococo goes further. Ranging freely, and influenced by the Carracci brothers, by Luca Giordano and even by Rubens, Tiepolo began to carry out his grandoise frescoes—the Colleoni Chapel at Bergamo (1733), Villa Byron (1734), the ceiling of the church of I Gesuati in Venice (1739), and the Palazzo Clerici in Milan (1740). Christian virtues and mythological figures, angels and Madonnas crowd ceilings and walls. Behind them limpid skies unfold in far-reaching splendour, scarcely disturbed by rose-coloured and grey-blue cirrus clouds. An inexhaustible joy in being alive led Tiepolo to create such masterpieces; and the Apollonian splendour of his light and colour finds no better comparison than with the mighty figurative empyrean of Paolo Veronese.

It is this sensitivity to light, this symphony of colour, that distinguishes Tiepolo and makes him so exceptional. When comparing him with great contemporary artists all over Europe Tiepolo's superiority in decorative work to a Coypel, a Lemoine, or even to Boucher himself is obvious. These artists, some more, some less, are tied to standards of late Baroque tradition. Tiepolo, on the other hand, moves freely and with originality in a realm of brilliant light and shows a genius for colour and a lively invention of forms only comparable with the great music of the period, which, in Venice, boasted such geniuses as Vivaldi.

Towards the middle of the century—elsewhere the current of the Rococo had come to an end—Tiepolo continued to produce great glowing masterpieces. In the Palazzo Labia a large ballroom is frescoed with complicated scenery of arcades, pediments, pierced windows and vaulting. High up on the architraves and round the curves of the arches, cut out against a clear sky, move divine beings and partly legendary figures, treated somewhat realistically, while in the centre, almost on the threshold of a grandiose spectacle in costume, the protagonists of the two largest paintings are introduced: the *Meeting of Antony and Cleopatra* and *The Banquet*. Who are these majestic figures in theatrical costume that is half 16th- and half 18th-century? Are they placed there for their colour? They are the dramatis personae from *rocaille* theatrical fantasy. Tiepolo knew how to lead them along the hazardous path of melodrama. And this formal courtly concourse was transformed by his brush into a great decorative scene— melodramatic, scenographic and palatial—interpreting, as no one else could, the spirit and demands of the age. There is poetic force of expression in every movement. One can find out how these decorative figures—apparently carefully calculated and measured—were created by studying certain of his drawings in outline, where the play of black and white produces, almost by magic, a whole scale of colour harmonies, from the blue and gold of the sky to the rosy flesh tints and the shot-silk effects of the clothes. The relationship between his drawings and the work he carried out in fresco and on canvas is complete. In the painting he rarely loses any of the freshness of the rough sketches, and the creator's touch is evident in fresco or canvas in forceful outlines which seem to aid the rapid flow of the brush over rich surfaces. One must remember, too, the decoration of his middle period, such as the overdoors in the Palazzo Barbaro in Venice, now dispersed in various collections. The lovely *Timoclea* from the Palazzo Barbaro, now in Washington, is a veritable casket of jewels with its fresh and gay brilliance.

Thus Tiepolo's fame spread everywhere and he approached the central episode in his life, a turning-point in the whole figurative culture of Europe. The prince bishop of Würzburg asked Tiepolo to fresco the central hall and great staircase of his beautiful palace, built by Neumann.

No meeting between the world of German Rococo

and the great Venetian decorator could have been more significant, and from it arose a host of imitators. Tiepolo was at Würzburg from 1750 to 1753, together with his sons, Giandomenico and Lorenzo, by now grown-up, his faithful assistants and trained in his school. The collaboration between the architect Neumann and the worker in stucco (Antonio Bossi) was an extremely happy one. In the grand staircase the dramatic and spectacular double ascending flights leading to a broad terrace find a complement in the transparency of Tiepolo's sky. Tiepolo takes up again in part the subject of the *Triumph of Apollo* in the Palazzo Clerici but finishes it with a fantastic portrayal of *The Four Quarters of the Earth*. All round are crowds of people from the bishop's court—ministers, generals, the architect, and self-portraits of Tiepolo and of his son Giandomenico.

Tiepolo's colour found in the *rocaille* architecture of Würzburg its most perfect setting. It is a grand symphony of exceptional glossy brilliance, skilfully using cool, limpid touches and diaphanous unreal clarity and contrasting this in figures where a sunlit warmth gives grace and softness. Würzburg astonishes and enraptures. It is not only Tiepolo's chief masterpiece; it also gives formidable proof of the decorative spirit of the European Rococo.

The imperial hall, narrating the history of Frederick Barbarossa, an ancestor of the prince bishop, is more delicate and more in the style of the characteristic work of southern Germany—white and gold stucco-work, transparent colour washes and graceful elegance. In the hall, enclosed by an arched vault in which open picturesque windows in the purest Bavarian Rococo, Tiepolo develops three principal themes, linked together by circles of minor figures. These are painted in tromp-l'oeil scenes all round the architectural features. Above, in a large oval, is *The Triumph of Frederick Barbarossa,* placed directly in front of the chariot of the sun. On the two sides are *The Investiture of Bishop Harold* and *The Wedding.* Figures in costume are shown against a background of enormous curtains drawn up at the sides. The painted architecture, the clothes, too, are once more in the 16th-century style of Paolo Veronese. It caused no surprise that the marriage of Frederick Barbarossa is blessed by the prince bishop Karl Philipp von Greiffenklau, Tiepolo's patron. For Tiepolo the historic theme had neither meaning nor value. The background and subject merely serve as pretexts for a gay decorative approach. To deck out his contemporaries in costume of a much earlier period was considered an ingenious invention and gained him even more sympathy from his noble patrons.

The work at Würzburg brought Tiepolo fame and money, but scarcely was his paint dry when the three painters were once again in Venice. From then onwards they formed a close artistic brotherhood as was formerly the custom in the golden age of art. Commissions were not lacking. In 1754 we know that he was painting the ceiling of the church of Sta Maria della Pietà with the *Triumph of the Faith* among choirs of angels and musical instruments—a reference to the excellent music given in that most lovely 18th-century church. He also painted at Nervesa, in the Villa Soderini, and then suddenly appeared in the Villa Valmarana, near Vicenza, which marked a new and most important stage in his activities (1757).

In the Palazzina of the Villa Valmarana, standing on the ridge of a hill overlooking Vicenza, Tiepolo frescoed a series of rooms with stories of Aeneas and Dido, stories from *Gerusalemme Liberata* (Tasso) and scenes on Olympus. His son Giandomenico worked in the Foresteria of the Villa. Never have two painters shown such similar technique but so different a spirit. Whereas Gian Battista is luminous and classical, Giandomenico has a nervous sensitivity and is often realistic; and whereas the elder man is oratorical and sure of himself, the younger shows a liking for the grotesque and is at times tortured. The two groups of frescoes in Valmarana—in the Palazzina and the Foresteria—reveal, therefore, in a strange way, the Tiepolos' secrets. Gradually the divergence in style became deeper, showing the gulf between two generations and two ideal worlds. In the Villa Valmarana, and increasingly as the years passed, Gian Battista sometimes yielded to his son's more realistic suggestions. This explains the tender feeling expressed in the farewells between Rinaldo and Armida and in the love of Medoro and Angelica; and then there is the occasional portrait, such as the *Procuratore* in the

Palazzo Querini in Venice. He looks almost sinister, swathed in a red cloak, his countenance livid in the nocturnal light, and this accentuates the arrogance of the outstretched hand on the table, painted with an astonishingly bold touch. At other times he produced caricatures expressing bitter unsmiling irony with a few quick strokes of sepia on white paper.

In comparison with the very individual work of his son Giandomenico, the elder Tiepolo's last pictures lose something of their classical brilliance, but they gain in profundity. From the Ca' Rezzonico to the Palazzo Canossa at Verona, from Este to Strà, he continued to carry out decoration on the grand scale with brilliance and enthusiasm. But the designs for his work vary less and less and sometimes give the impression of being backward-looking to a European culture that has turned away from the Rococo tradition. It would be difficult to guess, for example, that the rhetorical allegories of noble families, such as those of the Pisani family at Strà, are by his hand. When the king of Spain summoned him to fresco the palace in Madrid, Tiepolo seemed to have reached the limit of boredom. He handled his brushes with timeless and prodigious bravura, but he no longer had the creative felicity of his Würzburg work, even if it is reminiscent in subject-matter. Sometimes the ageing artist found opportunities more to his taste in certain small pictures, now mostly dispersed, in the church of Aranjuez, but preserved in sketches showing his great insight. These are canvases, modest in size, painted with thick brush-strokes and with no dazzling treatment, but inspired by inner religious fervour and human tenderness.

In 1770 Tiepolo died. He had developed his art in the first half of the 18th century during the high tide of Rococo and finished his life with albums of caricatures and easel paintings.

In order to complete the picture of Italian painting in the first half of the 18th century many other personalities should be mentioned. Sometimes it is difficult to fit them into the artistic background. In Italy, for example, there was an important group of realistic painters who specialised in portrait painting, in scenes from daily life or in landscape. The popular subjects of Ceruti, who worked in Lombardy between 1720 and 1740, show no affinity with the Rococo, whereas the subjects of the Venetian Pietro Longhi (1702-1782), in which the figures are usually in aristocratic dress and surroundings, recall the work of minor masters, followers of Watteau. Longhi probably knew their work from engravings and sketches and drew his inspiration from them. In hundreds of small pictures the whole of Venetian society from 1740 was passed in review by this urbane observant chronicler, and almost always the fineness of the design, the gay colours and the brilliance of his touch go back to origins common to Rococo.

Another aspect of the art of realism in Italy was that of landscape, whether in the presentation of scenes from town or country. In both cases the interest of the

18th-century, artist was directed towards the 'real'. His aim was accuracy, but naturally each artist's individual skill caused him to interpret what he saw in a different way. In Rome, for example, until the beginning of the 18th century views and episodes from town life predominated. The grandiose scenery of the Rome of antiquity, which more than ever interested artists because of the resurgent classical spirit, was often the chosen subject of the Dutchman van Wittel. He owes his importance to numerous imitators among the artists of the time. The 'portrait' of Rome as seen by him is naturally very faithful and accords with the way in which his education had taught him to see it. Nevertheless his light touch at times achieves a satisfactory balance between documentary precision and pictorial imagination.

His pupil, Gian Paolo Pannini from Piacenza, arrived in Rome in 1715 with a strong disposition towards architectural drawing and perspective derived from the Bibienas by whom he had been taught. He made his way by marrying the sister of Vleughels, director of the French Academy in Rome, and he was soon in the good graces of the powerful cardinals who still governed the artistic life of the city. In this way Pannini became the faithful chronicler and extoller of Rome, and his pictures bear the name of all the great events and most characteristic sites: the *Festivities for the Spanish Ambassador* in the Victoria and Albert Museum, London; the *Visit of Charles III to St Peter's* in Naples; the *Piazza Navona* in the Louve; and *Sta*

17. Giacomo Serpotta (1656-1732). Altar columns (detail) in the church of the Carmine, Palermo.

18. Giovanni Maria Morlaiter (1699-1781). *Adoration of the Magi. c.* 1730. Ca' Rezzonico, Venice.

19. Antonio Agostinelli. *Triumph of Bacchus*. Victoria and
Albert Museum, London.

20. L. Vanvitelli, Violani and Brunelli. *Diana the Huntress.*
Royal Park, Caserta.

21. Piedmont tapestry. *Cyrus Waging War against Artaxerxes.*
1750-1756. Palazzo Quirinale, Rome.

22. Piedmont school. Reception room, Palazzo Carignano, Turin.

23. Benedetto Alfieri (1700-1767). The Queen's cabinet, Royal Palace, Turin.

24. Piero Piffetti (1700-1777). Secretaire. Palazzo Quirinale, Rome.

25. Piero Piffetti (1700-1777). Pedestal with intarsia decoration. Palazzo Quirinale, Rome.

26. Venetian. Ballroom (*c.* 1753). Ca' Rezzonico, Venice.

27. Venetian. Little drawing-room with stucco-work and armchairs. c. 1750. Ca' Rezzonico, Venice.

28. Venetian. Drawing-room in green lacquer. Ca' Rezzonico, Venice.

29. Venetian. Carved armchair. Ca' Rezzonico. Venice.

30. Venetian. Lacquered commode. Ca' Rezzonico, Venice.

31. Venetian. Carved and gilded commode. Ca' Rezzonico, Venice.

32. Venetian. Gilded console table. Ca' Rezzonico, Venice.

33. Venetian. Gilded wall light. Ca' Rezzonico, Venice.

34. Venetian. Carved and gilded throne. Ca' Rezzonico,
Venice.

35. Venetian. Suite of furniture in green lacquer. Ca'
Rezzonico, Venice.

36. Venetian. Venetian bureau, surmounted by a cabinet with mirrored doors. Private collection, Milan.

37. Venetian. Chandelier from Murano (made by Briatti).

38. Venetian. Chandelier in wood and gilded metal. *c.* 1758.
Ca' Rezzonico, Venice.

39. Neapolitan. Sedan-chair of Charles of Bourbon. Capodimonte Museum, Naples.

40. Lombard. Coffee-pot. Castello Sforzesco, Milan.

41. Felice Clerici. Decorated plate. Castello Sforzesco, Milan.

42. Antonio Narciso Tomé. The Transparente altar, cathedral,
Toledo.

43. William Hogarth (1697-1764). *Mariage à la Mode* (detail).
1745. National Gallery, London.

44. Chelsea ware. A pair of candlesticks. London Museum, London.

45. Matthäus Daniel Pöppelmann (1662-1736). The Zwinger
(1722), Dresden.

46. François de Cuvilliés (1695-1768). Theatre (1751-1753).
Residenz, Munich.

47. François de Cuvilliés (1695-1768). Mirrored room in the
Amalienburg. Nymphenburg, near Munich.

48. Balthasar Neumann (1687-1753). The Residenz (c. 1753). Würzburg.

Maria Maggiore in the Palazzo Quirinale, Rome. The architectural harmony of these pictures and their perfect perspective drawing does not prevent the painter from achieving spectacular effects in the multi-coloured crowds, blue skies streaked with clouds, impressive buildings and noble ruins. Indeed, modern and antique Rome speak through his brush with extraordinary truth and felicity.

In these same years another great artist interpreted the Rome of antiquity, the Venetian Gianbattista Piranesi. He usually expressed himself in etchings, published in series from the middle of the century. *Studies in Architecture, Roman Antiquities, Prisons, Views of Rome* give a complete panorama by this great artist, who was also an architect, but who rejected the use of paint-brush and colour.

Piranesi's Rome has almost entirely disappeared, a Rome full of romantic nostalgia for that great civilisation surviving only in majestic but silent ruins. Intellectually Piranesi was deeply interested in the archaeological movements in Italy in the middle of the century at Herculaneum, Pompeii and Rome. The new theories were to give life to Neo-classicism. The German archaeologist Johann Joachim Winckelmann and the painter Raphael Mengs were ardent champions of Neo-classicism in their art and writing. For them true art could only mean Greek or Roman, perhaps slightly tainted by Renaissance artists. Any distortion, any invention that departed from classical orthodoxy was condemned as 'Baroque'. The ideal of art was to create 'perfect form', dictated by the canons of antiquity. There was a categorical, inflexible reaction against what Rococo had meant until then.

A taste for landscape and scenery developed, spread from Rome and assumed importance from early in the century. It was at this time that a stay in Rome began to be considered indispensable for the formation of young artists, whether foreign or Italian. Rome, too, had a great influence on the Italian Canaletto as well as on Vernet, Wilson, Hubert Robert and Fragonard.

Canaletto owed much of his interest in natural scenery to his knowledge of Roman art when, as a youth, he came in contact with the painting of van Wittel and Pannini. Until he was twenty he worked, as did his father and brother, in the theatre as a scene decorator. Plays such as Vivaldi's *Arsilda and Darius,* Chelleri's *Penelope* and Porta's *Agrippa* were produced between 1716 and 1718 against scenic backgrounds, and he could always find work in Venice where at least twenty theatres were open. But his true vocation was not to paint for so much a yard. Dutch painters such as Berckheyde, Backhuyser and even Vermeer himself, with their clean perspectives, attention to detail, yet with a painterly flow, enabled him to foresee greater possibilities in the use of colour.

The ruins of Rome, impressive perspectives, views of hills on which grew enormous leafy trees, the baked earth of gigantic walls in the foreground, the limpid sun of the south—everything contributed to set free a latent, although already individual, personality.

One has only to think of his earliest pictures (such as those formerly in the Liechtenstein Gallery in Vienna or in the Pillow Collection in Montreal) faithfully following the principles of perspective, but with lively backgrounds in which myriads of little touches of colour make his shimmering iridescence more brilliant and reveal an individual technique.

Canaletto's constant subject is Venice, *his* Venice, seen from every angle, patiently and minutely examined in its infinite and picturesque variety. Between 1730 and 1740 Canaletto finished the greater number of his Venetian views, those of the Grand Canal and of the city's enchanting prospects. His pictures left Venice twenty or thirty at a time, carrying with them the light of Italian skies and the colour of lagoon waters. In England, even today, at Woburn Abbey there is a series of thirty of his landscapes; and only recently has the Harvey collection, which had even more, been dispersed. Then in 1746 Canaletto's life was enriched by a new experience; for almost ten years he worked in England, painting landscapes for his patrons: the famous views of Eton, Alnwick and London, the brilliantly green park of Badminton, the vast perspectives of the Thames, crossed by bridges and peopled with boats, which must have reminded him of Venice. Quite wrongly this series is said to show a falling off in quality. On the contrary, it seems that Canaletto was developing his technique in the direction of a more abstract colour harmony and an unrestrained figurative richness.

Among Venetian landscape painters were Zais and Zuccarelli, skilled in portraying the gentle hills of the lower Alps and enlivening them with shepherds and shepherdesses spiritually nearly allied to those painted in the international Rococo style. It would be unjust too not to mention the gifted Francesco Guardi (1712-1793), although chronologically speaking he was only on the fringe of the Rococo. Brother of Gian Antonio, he concentrated almost entirely on landscape painting, if we exclude a few juvenile works in the field of religious art. He worked from the middle until almost the end of the 18th century: but his vision of nature was that of the great landscape artists of the age of Rococo.

At first Guardi followed Marco Ricci and Canaletto and developed in his *'capricci'* and in his views of Venice a gallery of pictures in which the subject, treated realistically, is illumined by brilliant scenic perspectives. His style is recognisable in imaginative fragmented brush-strokes that create an ephemeral world given over to fantasy and often withdrawn into melancholy. In his work the delightful interpretations of the Rococo attitude to landscape painting must be considered as at an end.

ITALIAN ROCOCO SCULPTURE

Italian sculpture of the early 18th century had many important regional schools but no genius. On the whole it did not succeed in freeing itself from the influence of Bernini and Algardi which bound it to motifs common to 17th-century figurative rhetoric. In Rome Rusconi personified above all the oratorical tendencies of the Algardi tradition in the superfluous draperies for his apostles in S. Giovanni in Laterano. Much more delicate, and not insensitive to the stylistic evolution of the Rococo, was the young Filippo della Valle (1696-1770) whose refined *Temperance* in S. Giovanni in Laterano was carved in 1734. Finally there was Pietro Bracci (1700-1773) with his picturesque, pleasing and expansive style. Sometimes, specially in such busts as that of Benedict XIV in Berlin, he achieved a naturalness of sharp modern flavour. Typically Rococo in its dramatic composition is the grandiose Trevi fountain, begun in 1732 by the architect Nicola Salvi. The statues that give it such animation form an anthology of the best artists working in Rome, particularly *Salubrità* (Health) and *Abbondanza* (Plenty) by della Valle, and the picturesque *Oceano* by Bracci.

In Naples the most talented sculptor was Antonio Corradini (1668-1752), whose chef-d'oeuvre is the Sansevero chapel. The virtuosity of his technique cannot hide an instinctive pictorial quality which is revealed in the delicate and tender modelling.

The only true sculptor from south Italy was Giacomo Serpotta (1656-1732) of Palermo, who worked almost exclusively in stucco. Following a tradition of Sicilian craftsmen he carried this art to a point very close to the language of the Rococo in refined elegance and dramatic effect. His best work was done in Palermo early in the 18th century: the oratory of S. Lorenzo was completed in 1706 and the church of S. Domenico in 1717. Influenced by the picturesque but classical sculpture of Raggi that he had studied in Rome, Serpotta created statues of expressive and pleasing form in which a thin vein of Hellenic purity is heightened by 18th-century sophistication.

It is in Venice and its surroundings that early 18th-century sculpture shows a unique significance, taking on definite Rococo accents. All the skilled cabinet-makers, such as Andrea Brustolon, who carried out decorative work in churches in Belluno and in Venetian palaces, and Giovanni Marchiori should be mentioned. But Gian Maria Morlaiter (1699-1781) is the most famous, a lively modeller of elegant figures in clay and terracotta, most of them conserved in the Ca' Rezzonico in Venice. These acquire interesting chromatic effects from the play of light and shade. 17th-century Italian tradition (still very much alive in Venice), Austrian Rococo and the brilliant fantasy of contemporary painting all unite to form his characteristic, humorous language.

INTERIOR DECORATION

When examining the development of the arts during the formation of the Rococo we have stressed the importance that the home came to assume as a centre for intimate family life. Its decoration had to be adapted to new functions. The home was no longer considered as a place for display, as were the houses of the nobility from the 16th century onwards, but as a genuine meeting-place for ordinary human beings, and it had to respect the need for comfort and the habits of daily life. The 18th century was a woman's epoch and the new surroundings seemed better adapted to refinement and intimacy than for pompous, bewigged gentlemen. Walls were decorated with *boiseries,* with stucco work and with rich but warm and cheerful material, while furniture was as comfortable as possible. There were gay ornaments in porcelain and coloured maiolica, rich in chromatic effects, and silver plate and sumptuous goldsmith's work. As always, almost the whole of Europe looked to the France of the regency or of Louis XV as its model. Often, however, national schools showed their independence with creations of refined and individual taste, and some of Italy's major achievements were in the field of Rococo furnishing.

While in France during the early Rococo period the fashion prevailed for walls to be decorated with *boiseries* or small panels, in Italy many ornamental elements of the Baroque period remained. All, however, took on a more delicate tone and were adapted to the smaller houses of the 18th century. Ceilings of noblemen's houses were often painted or frescoed, and thus, as has been seen, the great decorative schools, particularly in Venice and Naples, continued to flourish. Sumptuous and picturesque decoration in stucco was applied to walls and ceilings. Stucco, due to its malleability, allowed of most sensitive and delicate modelling and was easily adapted to figures from Rococo sculpture. Superb Roman interiors in palaces by Borromini or Bernini, or decorated by Pietro da Cortona, were enriched by stucco-work much later than the early 18th century; this was the case, too, in Palermo with Serpotta and in Milan with Bossi or Albertolli. The most typical *rocaille* stucco was in Venice, carried out in designs of light branches or foliage. Chefs-d'oeuvre of that typically 18th-century art are housed in the delightful surroundings of the Palazzo Venier, the Ca' Rezzonico and the Palazzo Albrizzi, all in Venice. The decoration of walls, too, with patterned and rich materials developed along individual lines in the Rococo period. Italian tapestry cannot stand comparison with the Beauvais, Gobelins and Aubusson tapestries. France had the advantage of the greatest artists to design the cartoons and of guilds boasting centuries-old traditions in weaving skill. Nevertheless, in the tapestry factories of Florence, Rome, Turin and Venice work of good quality was produced. In the Medici factories in Florence especially, elegant tapestry was woven up to 1737 from designs by Giovanni Sagrestani, Grifoni and Meucci; the subjects are for the most part Arcadian or mythological. In the Roman factories, under the patronage of Pope Clement XI, Procaccini and Signoret worked, often taking their subjects from groups of old tapestries in the papal collections but adapting them to the spirit of the Rococo. From 1737 King Carlo Emanuele III, the leading spirit in the artistic renaissance in Piedmont, was the patron of Francesco Demignot, whose workrooms were in Turin. There was also the tapestry of Dini. He used Beaumont's lively delicate cartoons for splendid scenes from the story of Cyrus, in the Palazzo Quirinale in Rome. Venetian tapestries, too, are usually by Dini and are of smaller size and ingenious in subject.

FURNITURE

The most highly valued and original furniture of the Rococo period is found specially in Piedmont and Venice. In Turin and in the castles of the duchy of Savoy furniture from the beginning of the 18th century took on the characteristics of *rocaille* with strong French overtones. The refurnishing of the great castles of Moncalieri and of Rivoli, the building of the Stupinigi and the interior decoration for the royal palace in Turin gave infinite opportunities to cabinetmakers and furniture designers. The style in wall decoration lies halfway towards that for French *boiseries,* with fine cornices outlining spaces and panels in wood or painted with arabesques; beautifully designed console tables with floral lines give élan to magnificent mirrors; tables and chairs have the curved

lines of Louis XV's reign, but the glowing sumptu-
ousness of gold is preferred to delicate lacquer. Towards the middle of the century the school of the
cabinetmaker Pietro Piffetti made a name for itself.
Piffetti became famous for his veneer and marquetry
in rare woods and bronze, and even in mother-of-
pearl, tortoiseshell and ivory. One admires the elegant
stylisation, expressed in the supple forms and
unpredictable caprices of *rocaille*.

The origins of Genoese furniture are similar, but
cabinetmakers of Parma and Emilia favoured a
heavier style of lacquered veneer and gilded carving,
above all in Louis XV taste. Their shapes were
rounded, comfortable, yet elegant. Roman and Neapolitan furniture often used veneering, then much in
favour, and work in precious woods; it is also rich in
the bronze ornamentation inherited from the 17th
century. Italian Rococo furniture in Venice has unmistakable individuality. There the cabinetmakers
started from a Baroque basis, with the furniture of
Andrea Brustolon, exquisite in workmanship and in
scenographic fantasy and veneered in walnut and
ebony, such as the examples in the Ca' Rezzonico.
Then the style changed to carved wood furniture,
often gilded and above all lacquered, but adopting,
it is true, the typical forms of French Rococo, although
even more elegant in refinement. Pictorial illustrations
in lacquer often showed the inventiveness of easel
pictures. The subjects preferred by 'painters' of Venetian furniture were chinoiserie and small Arcadian

figures and landscapes. They took as their models paintings by living Venetian artists and reached a high artistic level. A typical variety of Venetian furniture was described as 'poor man's lacquer'. This was made by sticking coloured paper on to wood mouldings and then varnishing it with a thin cast of colour, giving the illusion of absolute authenticity. The art of furniture-making in Venice in the 18th century was without doubt the most important in the whole of Italy and ended by employing artisans in more than three hundred workshops. These workshops employed more craftsmen than those of other Venetian crafts and specialised in making the wooden parts for furniture.

CERAMICS AND GLASS

The art of ceramics, most highly developed in German-speaking countries and in France, also in Italy found fruitful ground in Rococo forms. The factories of Venice, Capodimonte, Vinovo and Doccia are justly famous for their porcelain: and Bassano and the Marches for maiolica.

European porcelain, the result of the discovery of china clay in the Meissen factories, was made from the beginning of the century in Venice in the workshop of the Vezzi. Its inspiration was German but later it achieved independence through the work of the Cozzi. Delicately coloured tea and dinner services in the Ca' Rezzonico, little statuettes and chinoiserie are typical of their work. The Capodimonte factory specialised in coloured figurines in very white, almost transparent, soft paste. The most popular subjects were usually masked figures and peasants. The Savoyards, too, insisted on having their own factory at Vinovo. It flourished only in the second half of the century but was inspired by Rococo models. The Tuscan factory in Doccia limited itself in the end to ornamental decoration, specialising in friezes, cornices, looking-glasses, consoles and masked figures.

At Nove, near Bassano, the workshop of Antonibon produced the most delightful maiolica. He decorated his china with Arcadian subjects in relief. It was richly coloured and had a gay picturesque touch. Este also, near Padua, made typical table centrepieces in fine maiolica, the subjects and figures inspired by Rococo tradition.

In the field of china and glass, there is the characteristic glassware of Murano. The 18th century refined to the highest degree traditional Venetian virtuosity: glass assumed the appearance of precious stones, of chalcedony, of aventurine, and it imitated porcelain with a milky appearance or even lace by means of a fine network. Very ornate lamps are attributed to the Briata factory and in Venice the Ca' Rezzonico and the Palazzo Albrizzi still have some genuine examples. They have innumerable branches to hold candles and bunches of flowers in the most vivid colours imitating porcelain.

In the lavishly decorated halls of noblemen's palaces the grace, light, elegance and the refined aesthetic taste of the century are fully revealed in the infinite variety of objects quarried from the Rococo.

THE ROCOCO IN EUROPE

Except in France and Italy the Rococo did not have any important flowering in countries where the Baroque tradition of the 17th century had run aground in social and economic conservatism, deadening the stimulus of new ideas. Spain, for example, was held back from adopting Rococo motifs by her economic isolation and by the strong continuity of her Baroque tradition in decoration. In Salamanca, indeed, and in other less important centres, the 'plateresque' style of Churriguera prevailed. This is over-rich in external decoration but as regards structure it is basically linked in some degree to classicism. There was a *rocaille* flowering in the work of artists who followed: in Ribera's municipal library door in Madrid (1722), for example, and in the scenography of the 'Transparente' altar in Toledo cathedral, the work of Narciso Tomé. But that delicate and, at the same time, bizarre touch, that felicity and original talent of French and Italian Rococo, in harmony with a more carefree and materialistic conception of life, is fundamentally lacking from Spanish theatricality. Not even in the painting and sculpture of the Rococo period does

Spain show that she really understood what was going on in Europe: even Salzillo's polychrome figures in wood—the best that came out of Spain—have a pious Baroque rhetoric.

In England Rococo motifs developed quite independently and can be found mainly in the lesser arts, while architecture continued to follow orthodox Palladian style until it adopted a refined bourgeois Neo-classicism. Painting, too, which in the Rococo period produced the important artist William Hogarth (1697-1764), is not really influenced by *rocaille* forms. It is true that Hogarth draws inspiration from Watteau and his palette shows unexpected strength in its colour harmonies, without doubt learnt from the experiments of travelling Venetian artists such as Pellegrini. But his profound opposition to any real change is obvious in his choice of subjects. His pictures are so English in his attention to manners and dress, in his bitterly critical spirit and in his social involvement that one doubts whether it is possible to include him in the movement of European Rococo. We find, however, a more immediate contact in regard to porcelain; Chelsea ware, for example, often imitates Sèvres in colour, in capriciously asymmetrical modelling and in refined grace. We are often within the influence of Rococo biscuit with Longton Hall's little porcelain figures. This Staffordshire factory specialised in Arcadian subjects and in scenes of gallantry. Where Rococo taste really penetrated into Britain is with interior decoration and furniture.

Thomas Chippendale was in direct touch with the taste of Louis XV in furniture, which is all scrolls and volutes, and often influenced by chinoiserie, so fashionable at that time.

Germany is another European country in which Rococo assumed a dominating role in the development of the arts. In many regions, at that time each under a different government, forms highly valued in Paris were taken over by Germans at the beginning of the century and often developed with idiosyncratic independence.

One is aware of an unusual architectural flowering in Germany. For private houses German artists took French châteaux as their models, and for religious architecture they studied Roman churches. The influence of Borrominian Baroque resulted in an extraordinary animation in forms, picturesque fantasy and fertility of invention. In Dresden Pöppelmann created in the Zwinger a summer pavilion ideal for court fêtes and ceremonies, one of the chefs-d'oeuvre of European Rococo. In Prussia Knobelsdorff imitated the plans for Sans-Souci, with prospects opening on delightful gardens. In Bavaria François de Cuvilliés (not only in his name did he show French influence) built an architectural gem in his Residenz theatre, aglow with gilt and picturesque carving. His passion for *rocaille* was carried to its extreme in hundreds of pieces of furniture, armchairs, console tables and panels with bizarre carved scroll work. In other cities of Bavaria and Franconia Balthasar

Neumann (1687-1753) stands out. His finest works are the church of Vierzehnheiligen, with an undulating façade and its interior decorated in a symphony of white and gold, and the palace of the prince bishop of Würzburg, adorned with stuccos by Bossi and finally completed by Tiepolo's frescoes. In Vienna, too, architects developed their plans in conformity with the language of Rococo, particularly von Hildebrandt in his Belvedere (1721) enlivened with ornamental cornices, little cupolas and lateral pavilions.

Painters working in this artistic climate had to yield to the requirements of architecture. On the other hand painters got their way when it was a question of stars of the first magnitude such as Pellegrini in the palace of Mannheim or at Schleissheim, or Tiepolo at Würzburg. But it was usual for German or Austrian painters to adapt themselves to the exigencies of decoration. Decorators of ceilings such as Zimmermann, working at Nymphenburg, or Gran, painting the ceiling of the National Library in Vienna, were not highly considered. The Austrians Troger, Kremser-Schmidt and Maulbertsch were all, some more, some less, indebted to Venetian influence but very individual in their elaboration of a lively chromatic style, and their pungent yet urbane expressiveness in drawing has affinities with the Rococo.

In the field of sculpture German artists soon freed themselves from Bernini's influence. Permoser, working in Dresden, stood out, and they created, specially in Bavaria, new forms which range from painterly

49. Dominikus Zimmermann (1685-1766). Detail of the choir, pilgrimage church. Wies.

50. Johann Lucas von Hildebrandt (1668-1745). The Upper Belvedere (1721). Vienna.

51. Johann Baptist Zimmermann (1680-1758). Picture gallery (1728-1730). Residenz, Munich.

52. German. Large reception room in the Schaelzer Haus (1765-1770). Augsburg.

54. Daniel Gran (1694-1757). *Diana Rising to Olympus.*
Kunsthistorisches Museum, Vienna.

55. Johann Kremser-Schmidt (1718-1801). *The Assumption.* 1772. Kunsthistorisches Museum, Vienna.

56. Anton Maulbertsch (1724-1796). *The Marriage of the Virgin Mary.* 1755. Kunsthistorisches Museum, Vienna.

57. Ferdinand Tietz (1709-1777). *Harlequin*. Victoria and
Albert Museum, London.

58. Ignaz Günther (1725-1775). *An Angel in Flight. c.* 1745.
German National Museum, Nuremberg.

59. Egid Quirin Asam (1692-1750). Church of St Johannes Nepomuk (1733-1746), Munich.

60. Lorenzo Mattielli (1682/88-1748). *Daniel.* 1731. German National Museum, Nuremberg.

61. Meissen ware. *Lovers in Spanish Costume* (model by Kändler). 1740. State art collections, Dresden.

62. Meissen ware. *Harlequin* (model by Kändler). 1738.
German National Museum, Nuremberg.

63. Nymphenburg ware. *Lovers* (model by Bustelli). Bavarian National Museum, Munich.

sculpture by Tietz for the park at Veitschöchheim to the innumerable statues in wood carved and painted by Ignaz Günther (1725-1775), a real master of German Rococo. His Madonnas, his flying angels, his saints uplifted on clouds, the wood often gilded or silvered, accentuate with scintillating reflections the glowing light of church interiors. Sometimes his sculptures are simply painted white and only lightly gilded, giving chiaroscuro effects that enhance their expression of suffering. The dry and broken style of the attractive folding draperies is characteristic of this aspect of German Rococo and shakes off traditional academicism. Other sculptors who should be mentioned are Egid Quirin Asam for his church of St Johannes Nepomuk in Munich, and Lorenzo Mattielli, who decorated with strong and elegant sculpture the abbey of Melk on the Danube.

With such a wealth of new buildings their interior decoration and furnishing is clearly important, so much so that it is possible to speak of German Rococo in this field too. Many French cabinetmakers were in fact of German origin, such as Oeben and Riesener; but in Germany a national variety of Rococo furniture developed, laden with decoration, richly inlaid with ivory and precious materials and with bronze mounts. Large bureau-bookcases are typical, made by placing a cabinet with glass doors on a chest-of-drawers, the corners canted and the upper part surmounted with scrolls and flourishes. In Dresden lacquered furniture was made; in Munich Cuvilliés designed extravagant mirrors and console tables ornamented with branches and gilded scroll work.

The most individual talent of German artists of the Rococo is revealed perhaps in ceramics. In this they genuinely excelled all other Europeans. In 1709 the chemist Böttger had discovered the process by which porcelain could be made by melting down china clay. Translucent and smooth, Meissen porcelain was exactly like that of China, and its renown has been carried on to our own day. From 1710 Meissen factories produced objects of every kind—épergnes, small picture frames, chandeliers, plates, figures and portraits. Naturally it was not possible to keep the composition a secret, and soon every little German court felt that it must open its own factory. These gave work to vast numbers of craftsmen. Apart from Nymphenburg, which immediately rivalled Meissen, the porcelain of Höchst, Frankenthal, Ludwigsburg and Berlin made its appearance. Each factory had its own style which gradually changed, becoming more refined and the colours more delicate.

The porcelain was made from a model often prepared by a sculptor, and we have the names of some of them. Kändler created masterpieces of Meissen, famous for their pungency and vivacity of colour. At Nymphenburg F.A. Bustelli (1723-1763) from the Ticino created a world all his own, whimsical pretty figures drawn from life and particularly from the Commedia dell'Arte. All the characters from his exquisite scenes were improvisations on the love of

Cinzio and Isabella behind the back of the miser Pantaloon, on the jokes and intrigues of Harlequin, Pulcinella, Mezzetino and Scaramouche, Columbine and Pierrot. They offered Bustelli subjects to carry out in his graceful, piquant vein. The sculptural form with its lively line and picturesque lightness expresses as nothing else can a poetic world of smiling, unremembering happiness: the ideal world—that is the Rococo.

LIST OF ILLUSTRATIONS

1.   Antoine Watteau (1684-1721). *The Assembly in the Park. c.* 1717. Louvre, Paris. The composition is most attractive, the colours, shot through with flickers of light, are inspired by early floral ornament.

2.   François Boucher (1703-1770). *Diana Resting.* 1742. Louvre, Paris. A preference for the more fascinating and charming mythological characters is a feature of the Rococo. This picture can be taken as an example of a boudoir Venus.

3.   Gian Battista Piazzetta (1683-1754). *Idyll on the Shore. c.* 1740. Wallraf-Richartz Museum, Cologne. While the masters of Rococo decoration were enlivening princely houses all over Europe, Piazzetta in Venice confined himself to the best 17th-century traditions in painting, using strong yet richly varied colours and careful composition. Colour transforms light into a dazzling glow.

4.　Giovanni Antonio Pellegrini (1675-1741). *Marriage of the Elector William*. 1714. The palace, Schleissheim. One of a series of fourteen allegories with which the artist decorated the hall of the palace of Bensberg. A masterpiece of Pellegrini's mature period; the great 17th-century Italian tradition in painting is here revived in the attractive and ingenious forms of the Rococo manner.

5.　Giovanni Antonio Pellegrini (1675-1741). *Painting*. *c.* 1730. The Accademia, Venice. A mature work of Pellegrini, probably carried out after his return to Venice. The breaking up of the painted surfaces is typical and foreshadows the manner of Gian Antonio Guardi.

6.　Sebastiano Ricci (1659-1734). *Hercules and Cacus*. 1706-1707. Palazzo Marucelli, Florence. The mythological scene in which the shepherd Cacus is killed by Hercules is painted by Ricci in a wide Arcadian landscape, in early morning light. Typical Rococo magnificence.

7.   Rosalba Carriera (1675-1757). *Faustina Bordoni. c.* 1730. Ca' Rezzonico, Venice. In European society Rosalba Carriera attracted the very greatest attention. Her portraits, well drawn and voluptuously pretty, made her famous in the courts of Vienna, Paris and Dresden.

8.   Louis Tocqué (1696-1772). *The Comtesse Loménie de Brienne.* 1737. Musée des Beaux-Arts, Strasbourg. Son-in-law of the famous Nattier, court portrait painter at the height of the Rococo period. Tocqué seeks to portray fleeting expressions and to give a subtle interpretation of character.

9.   Gian Battista Tiepolo (1696-1770). *Rinaldo Charmed by Armida. c.* 1753. Alte Pinakothek, Munich. While frescoing the palace at Würzburg, Tiepolo succeeded in producing one of the outstanding paintings of the Rococo period. As well as the picture here reproduced he painted numerous canvases with scintillating freshness of colour.

10. Francesco Guardi (1712-1793). *The Convent Parlour.* *c.* 1750. Ca' Rezzonico, Venice. Francesco Guardi first learnt painting in the studio of his brother, Gian Antonio. It is difficult to attribute to Francesco some of his early work, so greatly does it resemble his brother's. There are even doubts about *The Convent Parlour,* but it is thought to be by him because of the drawing and the realism of the light.

11. Gian Antonio Guardi (1699-1760). *Tobit and his Wife in Prayer* (detail). *c.* 1749. Church of the Arcangelo Raffaelo, Venice. The organ balcony of the church is decorated with five incidents in the story of Tobit's son Tobias and the angel, and with angels making music. This is a masterpiece of the kind of painting which, beginning with Ricci and Pellegrini, continued until the middle of the century.

12. Gian Battista Tiepolo (1696-1770). The Orlando Furioso Room (1757), Villa Valmarana, Vicenza. In the middle of the 18th century sometimes even frescoes were subjected to the requirements of Rococo decoration. This is the case with Tiepolo's paintings in the Valmarana where his illustrations for the story of Angelica and Medoro were placed in ornate frames (the work of Mengozzi-Colonna), but they do not distract from Tiepolo's dazzling palette.

13.   Pietro Longhi (1702-1782). *The Charlatan.* 1757. Ca'
Rezzonico, Venice. Longhi painted familiar surroundings and
genre pictures; his interiors have a vivacious atmosphere
worthy of a Dutch painter and a pungent, yet good-humoured,
wit in the manner of Goldoni.

14.   Giovan Paolo Pannini (1692-1765). *Charles III Visiting
St Peter's.* 1745. Capodimonte Museum, Naples. A master in
portraying episodes from real life in 18th-century Rome,
Pannini knew how to orchestrate his gay, animated crowds
in order to give a lively picture of the city.

15.   Antonio Canal, known as Canaletto (1697-1768). *The
Piazza of S. Marco.* National Gallery of Art, Washington.18th-
century Venice comes out with extraordinary liveliness from
Canaletto's canvases, and he preserves the cheerful colour
schemes and lively gaiety of the Rococo period. This picture
encloses within a wide-angled perspective an extended view
of Venice. He used an optical device (camera obscura) to
help him with his drawings.

16. Francesco Guardi (1712-1793). *The Little Piazza of S. Marco. c.* 1765. Ca' d'Oro, Venice. In his role of townscape painter Guardi took his inspiration as regards composition from Canaletto. But he departed from him profoundly in his emphasis on and rendering of the picturesque, being much less precise topographically. His colour harmonies are rich and suggestive of mystery.

17. Giacomo Serpotta (1656-1732). Altar columns (detail) in the church of the Carmine, Palermo. Serpotta of Palermo raised to new dignity the tradition of Sicilian stucco-work. This elaborate decoration, with clusters of flowers and fruit, and human figures, interprets with a lightness that is wholly *rocaille* a theme that goes back to classical antiquity.

18. Giovanni Maria Morlaiter (1699-1781). *Adoration of the Magi. c.* 1730. Ca' Rezzonica, Venice. Venetian by birth, Morlaiter's family came from the Upper Adige and had probably had contacts with sculpture north of the Alps. His sculptural style shows the influence of German Rococo, while in the subtle modelling of the background he is seeking typically Venetian pictorial effects.

19.   Antonio Agostinelli. *Triumph of Bacchus.* Victoria and Albert Museum, London. This group shows clearly that it belongs to the Rococo period. Its sculptural form is superbly realised in a group instinct with life and movement.

20.   L. Vanvitelli, Violani and Brunelli. *Diana the Huntress.* Royal Park, Caserta. The royal park is enlivened by an extraordinary group of figures placed in a cleverly chosen setting. The effect is theatrical and is typical of the Rococo period.

21.   Piedmont. Tapestry. *Cyrus Waging War against Artaxerxes.* 1750-1756. Palazzo Quirinale, Rome. Forms one of a series of the Life of Cyrus. The cartoons were executed by Beaumont and carried out by the tapestry-weavers Demignot and Dini at the Royal Turin Factory.

22. Piedmont school. Reception room, Palazzo Carignano, Turin. A taste for richness, especially in the extravagantly decorated looking-glasses and mouldings with gilded scrolls, is characteristic of this interior in typical Piedmont Rococo.

23. Benedetto Alfieri (1700-1767). The Queen's cabinet, royal palace, Turin. In Piedmont the architecture of interiors is directly influenced by French taste. The royal palace in Turin is sumptuously furnished by Piffetti and the decoration is carried out with great refinement.

24. Piero Piffetti (1700-1777). Secretaire. Palazzo Quirinale, Rome. The creations of this cabinet maker add to Louis XV elegance a gay decoration in multi-coloured marquetry. Mother-of-pearl, bone, ivory and rare woods have been used to obtain the most brilliant results.

25.   Piero Piffetti (1700-1777). Pedestal with intarsia decoration. Palazzo Quirinale, Rome. This comes from the royal palace in Turin where in the middle of the 18th century there were a number of pieces of furniture of great decorative beauty.

26.   Venetian. Ballroom. (*c.* 1753), Ca' Rezzonico, Venice. The reception hall used for festivities in the Ca' Rezzonico takes up two storeys and is one of the most impressive in the city. The picturesque decoration carried out in fresco is the work of Giambattista Crosato and was completed in 1753 when the Rezzonico family first came to live in the palace. It was furnished with armchairs and divans placed along the walls.

27.   Venetian. Little drawing-room with stucco-work and armchairs. *c.* 1750. Ca' Rezzonico, Venice. This small drawing-room came from the Palazzo Calbo Crotta and was reconstructed in the Ca' Rezzonico. It is one of the rare examples of 18th-century painted stucco-work. The elegant taste in decoration and the gay lightness of the modelling make it a masterpiece.

28. Venetian. Drawing-room in green lacquer. Ca' Rezzonico, Venice. The commode with the tall mirror in a carved frame, the armchairs with curved legs, the cornices over the door with gilded carving from the Palazzo Calbo Crotta form one of the most typical existing Venetian Rococo ensembles.

29. Venetian. Carved armchair. Ca' Rezzonico, Venice. The 18th-century Venetian style in furniture adapted itself to the current fashions of the Rococo. Armchairs imitated French chairs of Louis XV's time. Venetian lacquer, made by spreading a varnish over genuine paint, has a fresh transparency.

30. Venetian. Lacquered commode. Ca' Rezzonico, Venice. The commode stands in the drawing-room from the Palazzo Calbo Crotta and is a masterpiece of Venetian lacquer: the design, with the bunches of brightly coloured flowers, stresses its pictorial aspect more than its craftsmanship.

31. Venetian. Carved and gilded commode. Ca' Rezzonico, Venice. Part of the furnishing of a Martinengo drawing-room of the early 18th century. A rare specimen which unites an imposing appearance with delicacy in execution.

32. Venetian. Gilded console table. Ca' Rezzonico, Venice. Very rich carving of swags of flowers make this side-table a piece of great character. The floral themes of the Rococo receive highly imaginative treatment at the hands of mid 18th-century Venetian craftsmen.

33. Venetian. Gilded wall light. Ca' Rezzonico, Venice. A large number of wood-carvers, lacquer-workers and gilders were employed in Venice. Mirrors, too, were made by glass-workers from Murano and the frames were carved with elegant designs.

34.   Venetian. Carved and gilded throne. Ca' Rezzonico, Venice. At times the taste for Venetian furniture results in the reproduction of archaic models, as in this throne which is enriched, nevertheless, by designs in Rococo taste.

35.   Venetian. Suite of furniture in green lacquer. Ca' Rezzonico, Venice. Effective imitations of chinoiserie furniture also flourished in Venice. This drawing-room in the Ca' Rezzonico in green lacquer and with figures in gold is a masterpiece. Chinoiserie was a characteristic of decorative Rococo.

36.   Venetian. Venetian bureau surmounted by a cabinet with mirrored doors. Private collection, Milan. A chest of drawers with sloping top, surmounted by a cabinet with mirrored doors. Such pieces of furniture by their imposing elegance give distinction to a drawing-room.

37.   Venetian. Chandelier from Murano (made by Briatti). Twenty branches of blown glass, enlivened by coloured enamelled ornaments, give this chandelier decorative elegance.

38.   Venetian. Chandelier in wood and gilded metal. *c.* 1758. Ca' Rezzonico, Venice. Made originally to light the palace ballroom, this chandelier imitates the lightness of glass by its fantasy in modelling and the brilliance of the gilding.

39.   Neapolitan. Sedan-chair of Charles of Bourbon. Capo-dimonte Museum, Naples. Rich example of carving in relief in the Spanish tradition in vogue at the court of Naples.

40. Lombard. Coffee-pot. Castello Sforzesco, Milan. The manufacture of maiolica in Lombardy in the 18th century produced, specially in Clerici's work, fine ware with an oriental bias and a very effective touch of observation. The landscape and birds in flight on his coffee-pot are an example.

41. Felice Clerici. Decorated plate. Castello Sforzesco, Milan. Clerici's work is distinguished by great elegance in the shapes and a certain vivacious and plebeian flavour in the design. Here, between trees in an imaginary landscape, wander charming little realistic figures.

42. Antonio Narciso Tomé. The Transparente altar, cathedral, Toledo. Composed of an incredible assortment of wood, marble, stucco and gilded bronze, this typically Spanish altar recreates 'plateresque Baroque' in pure Rococo.

43.   William Hogarth (1697-1764). *Marriage à la Mode* (detail). 1745. National Gallery, London. Hogarth often painted series of pictures on themes satirising English society. This picture is one of the *Marriage à la Mode* series. Where the Rococo idiom affects Hogarth is in elegant design and in his iridescent, vibrant and glowing colours.

44.   Chelsea ware. A pair of candlesticks. London Museum, London. The Chelsea factory, founded in 1747, was among the most active in making soft-paste porcelain. Fanciful figures are enriched by gay floral decoration in the Rococo taste.

45.   Matthäus Daniel Pöppelmann (1662-1736). The Zwinger (1722), Dresden. This summer pavilion for festivities and ceremonies, constructed on horizontal lines in order to create, with its symmetrical wings, a vast elegant piazza, was a model for many palaces of the Rococo period, specially in north Germany. The rich sculpture that decorates it is by Permoser.

46. François de Cuvilliés (1695-1768). Theatre (1751-
1753), Residenz, Munich. The finest existing example of an
18th-century theatre in the Rococo style. Its small size and
delicate architectural modelling throw into relief the sumptuous
decoration in white and gold.

47. François de Cuvilliés (1695-1768). Mirrored room in the
Amalienburg, Nymphenburg, near Munich. In the charming
little palace in the Nymphenburg park the stucco decoration
by J. B. Zimmermann and the sculpture by F. Dietrich create an
atmosphere of lightness and grace.

48. Balthasar Neumann (1687-1753). The Residenz (*c.*
1753), Würzburg. Neumann's masterpiece, begun in 1719 and
finished—as regards the wall structure—in 1733. The decoration was not completed until 1753. Architecturally the palace
shows signs of the restrained influence of the last phase of
Rococo.

49. Dominikus Zimmermann (1685-1766). Detail of the choir, pilgrimage church, Wies. In the church of Wies, Zimmermann's chef-d'oeuvre, he embellished the entire décor with extravagant Rococo moulding.

50. Johann Lucas von Hildebrandt (1668-1745). The Upper Belvedere (1721), Vienna. Built by Prince Eugène of Savoy, this summer residence dominates Vienna from the top of a hill. Its'lively appearance is achieved by the central masses of the building, by the strongly emphasised corner pavilions and by the exuberant fantasy of the decoration over the windows.

51. Johann Baptist Zimmermann (1680-1758). Picture gallery (1728-1730), Residenz, Munich. Chef-d'oeuvre of stucco-work by the most famous Bavarian working in Nymphenburg. German stucco-work differs from that of Venice and consists of separate gilded scrolls scattered on a flat white background.

52.   German. Large reception room in the Schaelzer Haus (1765-1770), Augsburg. The reception rooms in German palaces in the middle of the 18th century tend towards dazzling ostentation, such as gilded stucco decorations on a white background with a lavish use of mirrors and chandeliers.

53.   German. Music room. Thüringer Museum, Eisenach. A polygonal room plan with broken wall surfaces is characteristic of German Rococo. This makes it possible to enliven walls with a stucco decoration of floral branches producing pseudo-natural effects.

54.   Daniel Gran (1694-1757). *Diana Rising to Olympus.* Kunsthistorisches Museum, Vienna. Apollo introduces Diana to the Olympians in a joyous swirl of flying figures; at the sides hunting scenes and allegories of the goddess. In this mature work Daniel Gran takes themes from traditional Roman decoration and treats them with the heightened colours of the Rococo.

55. Johann Kremser-Schmidt (1718-1801). *The Assumption.* 1772. Kunsthistorisches Museum, Vienna. Originally painted for an altar in the parish church of Melk. A native of Krems (whence the name by which he is best known), Schmidt was the Austrian painter who most nearly resembled the Venetians. He was in fact a close follower of Diziani, adding rich, harmonious colour to the latter's extravagant Rococo compositions.

56. Anton Maulbertsch (1724-1796). *The Marriage of the Virgin Mary.* 1755. Kunsthistorisches Museum, Vienna. This is the sketch for the reredos in the church of Maria Treu in Vienna. Brought up on examples of late Italian Baroque, Maulbertsch never lost an unmistakable Nordic character. He expresses his nervous sensibility in flickering colour and tremors of light. Austrian Rococo finds its highest expression in his work.

57. Ferdinand Tietz (1709-1777). *Harlequin.* Victoria and Albert Museum, London. Model in wood for one of the garden statues that won for Tietz a prominent position among German decorators in the most lively and inventive period of the Rococo.

58.   Ignaz Günther (1725-1775). *An Angel in Flight. c.* 1745. German National Museum, Nuremberg. Among the sculptors of the middle of the 18th century in Germany, Günther shows an inspiration more obviously in sympathy with international Rococo. His dancing angels (such as this model in wood for the altar of the Knöbel chapel in Munich) and his draped saints have an atmosphere of lightness, emphasised by his elegant use of colouring.

59.   Egid Quirin Asam (1692-1750). Church of St Johannes Nepomuk (1733-1746), Munich. This building represents the masterpiece of Rococo religious architecture in Munich. The façade, curvilinear and extravagant in ornament, is elaborated with sculptural conceits; the interior is a phantasmagoria of light and reflections.

60.   Lorenzo Mattielli (1682/88-1748). *Daniel.* 1731. German National Museum, Nuremberg. Born in Ticino, Mattielli was in Vienna in 1712 and was in touch with the first sculptors of the German Rococo. He moved to Dresden in 1740 where he decorated churches and palaces in the light and picturesque style of the statue in wood reproduced here. It was a small model for the altar in the church of Melk.

61. Meissen ware. *Lovers in Spanish Costume* (model by Kändler). 1740. State art collections, Dresden. After the discovery of porcelain by the chemist Böttger, the Meissen factory was founded. Models by Joachim Kändler were used. The most delicate inventive grace inspires these figures, chefs-d'oeuvre of the Rococo.

62. Meissen ware. *Harlequin* (model by Kändler). 1738. German National Museum, Nuremberg. Many of the porcelain figurines designed by Kändler illustrate characters from the Commedia dell'Arte, then celebrated throughout Europe through the performances of travelling companies.

63. Nymphenburg ware. *Lovers* (model by Bustelli). Bavarian National Museum, Munich. A native of Ticino, Francesco Antonio Bustelli established himself in Munich in 1754 as designer for Nymphenburg ware. His little figures, some of which are taken from the Commedia dell'Arte, are delicate ingenious creations of European Rococo.